How to File Your Own Bankruptcy

The Step-by-Step Handbook to Filing Your Own Bankruptcy Petition

STEPHEN LEE

ISBN 978-1-68570-614-2 (paperback)
ISBN 978-1-68570-615-9 (digital)

Christian Faith Publishing
832 Park Avenue
Meadville, PA 16335
www.christianfaithpublishing.com

Printed in the United States of America

CONTENTS

INTRODUCTION

If you're reading this book, it's a good chance you have thought about filing bankruptcy, or you are thinking about filing bankruptcy.

Bankruptcy helps people who can no longer pay their debts get a fresh start.

If you are facing financial hardship and want a fresh start, this is a step-by-step guide that will help you file your own bankruptcy petition, if you are financially overwhelmed, want a fresh start, and can't afford an attorney to help you.

I'll keep it simple.

Chapter 1

Pro Se

What is Pro Se?

Latin meaning on one's own behalf or for himself. This typically refers to an individual who represents oneself in court. For example, an indigent but educated litigant who decides to forgo hiring a lawyer he cannot afford and be self-represented in court (Black's Law Dictionary, second edition).

One proceeding for himself and on their own behalf in person (Black's Law Dictionary, fourth edition).

CHAPTER 2

Chapter 7 or Chapter 13 Bankruptcy

There are two primary forms of federal bankruptcy for an individual or couple to file: one is Chapter 7 bankruptcy, and the other is a Chapter 13 bankruptcy.

A Chapter 13 bankruptcy is based on a proposed repayment plan submitted with your bankruptcy petition. This plan must show, after reasonable monthly expenses have been paid, how much money will you have leftover to put toward your outstanding bills. Priority claims such as taxes and back child support must be paid in full; unsecured debts like credit card debt and medical bills are paid in part.

The repayment plan must be made in good faith, and all disposable income must be paid into the plan for at least three years. Your plan payments will be withdrawn directly from your wages.

In a Chapter 7 bankruptcy filing, the individual or couple is seeking a clean slate; that is, you will be asking the court to wipe out all of your consumer debt.

Consumer debt means phone bills, utility bills, credit card bills, and medical bills.

Once you have filed your bankruptcy petition with the bankruptcy court, an automatic stay immediately goes into effect. Creditors cannot sue, garnish your wages, repossess property, or try to collect from you. In some cases, creditors cannot evict you if you rent. The stay will also stop any foreclosure proceedings.

Although there is a stay in effect during your pending bankruptcy petition, if you intend on keeping secured debts such as house or car after you receive your bankruptcy discharge, you will need to keep making payments before and after you receive a bankruptcy discharge.

Also, although such debts as back child support, alimony, student loans, taxes, fines, and penalties including traffic tickets and criminal restitution are also stayed during your pending bankruptcy petition, those types of debts cannot be discharged, and you are responsible for repaying these types of debts after your discharge.

It is up to the individual or couple to decide which plan is better for them.

This book is a step-by-step guide on filing your own Chapter 7 bankruptcy petition.

I'm going to keep it simple.

CHAPTER 3

Getting Started

If you have gotten this far, it means you or you and your spouse have decided on filing a Chapter 7 bankruptcy petition.

The first thing you or you and your spouse need to do is find the US district court/US bankruptcy court in the state or US territory in which you reside; you can go to Appendix A in the back of the this book; if you can't find the location of the US district court/US bankruptcy court in your area, you can go to www.uscourts.gov/court-locater and put in the requested information.

Once at your court's website, go to the link that says forms, and download the following forms: B-101, B-101A, B-101B, B-103A, B-103B, B-106DEC, B-106SUM, B-106A/B, B-106C, B-106D, B-106E/F, B-106G, B-106H, B-106I, B-106J, B-106J-2, B-107, B-108, B-119, B-121, B-122A-1, B-122A-1SUPP, B-122A-2.

CHAPTER 4

How to Obtain Your Credit Reports

Your credit reports contain the information about your creditors, specifically the name and addresses of your creditors.

Be sure to have all your bills together in case a particular creditor is not listed in your credit report; you can list the information that is on that bill in your bankruptcy petition. There are three major credit bureaus; they are as follows:

1. Equifax
2. Experian
3. TransUnion

To get a free copy of all three of your credit reports, go to www. annualcreditreport.com; you can get a free copy of each of your three credit reports once a year.

When you go to www.annualcreditreport.com, be sure you have access to a working printer loaded with paper and ready to print out copies of your credit report.

Once you leave the Equifax link, go to the Experian link; that's your one free copy for the year, so if you don't print out your copy while you're at Equifax, you will have to pay if you want a copy of that Equifax report.

When filling out your bankruptcy petition, the section you want to focus on is the "adverse accounts" section of your credit reports; that section lists your creditors and there addresses.

CHAPTER 5

Credit Counseling Certificate

You are required to take two courses regarding your finances and file proof-of-completion certificates for each course with the US bankruptcy court.

The first certificate is a credit-counseling certificate, and getting this certificate is a mandatory requirement. You must get this credit-counseling certificate within 180 days (six months) before you file your bankruptcy petition.

When you fill out your Bankruptcy Form 101, there is a section on that form where you have to explain your efforts to receive a briefing about credit counseling.

To take your credit-counseling course and obtain your credit-counseling certificate, you have to find an approved credit-counseling agency that offers courses online or by phone.

You can go to your bankruptcy court's website in Appendix A in the back of this book; click on the link credit-counseling course to find an agency that offers online or phone courses in your area or Appendix D.

Some agencies offer both the credit-counseling course and the second course you'll have to take after you file your bankruptcy petition—the personal financial management course. Find out if they offer a discount for paying for both courses at the same time. If you choose to pay for both courses at the same time, you only need to take the credit-counseling course and get that certificate to file your bankruptcy petition.

You'll need a printer or access to a printer in order to print out your completion certificate. Also some US bankruptcy courts provide Pro Se filers with computer access check with your bankruptcy court.

Once you print out your completion certificate for your credit-counseling certificate, you can go back into your account later to take the personal financial management course.

CHAPTER 6

Ready to Fill Out Bankruptcy Forms

You've downloaded your bankruptcy forms, you have all of your three free credit reports or at least one or two of them, and you have a copy of your credit-counseling certificate; you are now ready to start filling out your bankruptcy forms.

I'm going to take you step-by-step through every form you need to fill out in order to file your own bankruptcy petition.

I'm going to keep it simple.

CHAPTER 7

Voluntary Petition: Form B-101

At the top of every form, you're going to fill out for your bankruptcy petition; it states the following:

United States Bankruptcy Court for the:
—————District of—————

Some states have more than one district, for example, Eastern, Western, Northern, Southern, Central, or Middle. You have to identify what district you live in, as that is the US bankruptcy court you must file your petition in.

You can go to Appendix A in the back of this book or www. UScourts.gov/court-locater, if you don't know what district covers the county you live in. Once you know your district, you put that information in the first blank. For example, you're located in a county covered by the Northern District of Alabama; you would put Northern District of Alabama.

Because you are just filing your case, you won't have a case number, so just put N/A on that blank. In the chapter you are filing under, check Chapter 7 on each form.

In part 1, read each question carefully, and provide the requested information. In part 2, read each question carefully, and provide the requested information. If you checked to pay the filing fee in installments, you will need to fill out Form B-103A. If you requested the filing fee to be waived, you will need to fill out Form B-103B. Also in part 2, do you rent your residence? If you checked no, go to part 3.

If you checked yes and your landlord has obtained an eviction judgment against you before you filed your bankruptcy petition and you want to stay in your residence, you have to fill out Form B-101A.

If your landlord has obtained an eviction judgment against you before you filed your bankruptcy petition and you have moved or don't want to stay in your residence, you don't have to fill out Form B-101A.

In parts 3 and 4, read each question carefully, and provide the requested information. In part 5, read each question carefully, and provide the requested information about your credit counseling. If you have your completion certificate, attach a copy to your petition.

In part 6, read each question carefully, and provide the requested information. For how many creditors do you estimate that you owe, add up all your creditors, estimate of your assets is what you currently own, and an estimate of your liabilities is what you owe your creditors.

In part 7, read carefully, sign, and date. If you are representing yourself Pro Se, just put N/A in the attorney section. Then read and fill out the section for those filing bankruptcy without an attorney.

CHAPTER 8

Initial Statement about and Eviction Judgment Against You: Form B-101A

You only need this form if at the time you file your bankruptcy petition you rent your residence and your landlord has obtained a judgment in an eviction action against you and you wish to stay in your residence.

If that's your situation, read the form carefully, specifically the certification section of the form. If you checked both boxes in the certification section, your eviction will be stayed for thirty days after you file your bankruptcy petition, as long as you pay the bankruptcy clerk one-month rent.

If you want to stay in your residence past the first thirty days after you file your bankruptcy petition and continue to receive the protection of the automatic stay, you will have to pay your entire delinquent rent amount to your landlord, as stated in the eviction judgment before the first thirty-day period ends.

If at the time you file your bankruptcy petition you rent your residence but your landlord has not attempted to evict you or obtained an eviction judgment against you, you do not need to fill out Form B-101A.

CHAPTER 9

Statement about Payment of an Eviction Judgment Against You: Form B-101B

You only need this form if at the time you filed your bankruptcy petition you rent your residence and your landlord has obtained a judgment in an eviction action against you, you wish to stay in your residence, and you filled out Form B-101A. If that's your situation, read Form B-101B carefully, and fill it out.

If at the time you file your bankruptcy petition you rent your residence but your landlord has not attempted to evict you or obtained an eviction judgment against you, you do not need to fill out Form B-101A or Form B-101B.

CHAPTER 10

Application for Individuals to Pay the Filing Fee in Installments: Form B-103A

If you cannot pay the filing fee, currently $335.00, at the time you file your bankruptcy petition, you can ask the court to be allowed to pay the filing fee in installments.

You propose to the court how you will pay the $335.00 filing fee in four payments within 120 days of your filing your bankruptcy petition. For example:

$100.00 with the filing of the petition or on or before 00/00/00
$100.00 on or before_____
$50.00 on or before_____
$85.00 on or before_____

On the order approving payment of filing fee in installments, only fill out top portion of the form; the court will fill out the bottom portion of the form.

If you fill out Form B-103A, requesting to pay your filing fee in installments, you do not need to fill out Form B-103B, requesting to have filing fee waived. You can only fill out one form in regard to paying the filing fee if it is not paid in full when you file your bankruptcy petition.

CHAPTER 11

Application to Have the Chapter 7 Filing Fee Waived: Form B-103B

If you did not pay the filing fee in full at the time you filed your bankruptcy petition and you did not fill out Form B-103A, requesting to pay the filing fee in installments, you can fill out Form B-103B to request to have the filing fee waived.

If you are requesting to have the filing fee waived, you need to complete Form B-106A/B Schedule A/B: Property, Form B-106I Schedule I: Your Income, Form B-106J Schedule J: Your Expenses. In part 1, read each question carefully, and have Form B-106J Schedule I and Form B-106J Schedule J filled out and ready to use to answer your questions.

In part 2, read each question carefully and have your Schedules I and J filled out and ready to use to answer your questions.

In part 3, read each question carefully, and have Form B-106A/B Schedule A/B: Property filled out and ready to use to answer your questions.

In part 4, read each question carefully, and check the appropriate boxes, sign, and date.

On the order on the application to have the Chapter 7 filing fee waived, just fill out the top portion of that form; the court will fill out the bottom portion of the form.

CHAPTER 12

Schedule A/B: Property— Form B-106A/B

Read Schedule A/B carefully; in part 1, if you own any residence land or real estate, answer the questions in that section. If you own no residence, land, or real estate, check no, and go to part 2.

In part 2, describe any vehicles you may have and their current value. Because of depreciation value of any type of property listed in part 2, those older than three years old will have little or no value. What is the current blue book value at the time you file your bankruptcy petition?

In part 3, describe your personal and household items. Again because of depreciation value of any type of property listed in part 3, those older than two years old will have little or no value.

For example, if you just brought a new major appliance, a washer and a dryer, six months to one year before you filed bankruptcy for $900.00, it would not be worth $900.00 but would have some value. If they were over one year old, it would have little or no value.

In part 4, describe your financial assets. In part 5, describe any business-related property you own or have an interest in. For example, do you own or have an interest in a gas station? If so anything associated with your ownership or interest in that gas station has to be listed, and your ownership or interest in such property would also have to be listed in part 1.

In part 6, describe any farm or commercial fishing-related property you own or have an interest in. If none check no, and go to part 7. In part 7, describe all property you own or have an interest in that's not listed in parts 1–6. If none check no; go to part 8. In part 8, total up all the personal property from part 1 to part 7.

CHAPTER 13

Schedule C: The Property You Claim as Exempt—Form B-106C

An exemption is a law that allows you to keep certain property. The law allows you to keep certain property as exempt; exempt property cannot be sold to pay your creditors. You must list all your property from your Schedule A/B that you claim as exempt.

Read Schedule C carefully; in part 1, you have to indicate which set of exemptions you are claiming your property falls under, a state or federal exemption.

In some states, you can choose to use either your state exemptions or federal exemption.

In some states, you can choose only your state exemptions if your state does not recognize the federal exemptions.

For example, if you live in Alabama, the state of Alabama does not recognize the federal exemptions, so in part 1, number 1, you could only check the first box.

If you live in a state that allows you to choose either your state exemptions or federal exemptions, you can check either one box or the other in part 1, number 1.

You cannot mix or match federal and state exemptions. You have to pick one or the other. To decide if you want to use your state exemptions or federal exemptions, see Appendix B in the back of this book.

Once you have decided which exemption you can or want to use, you list that exemption on your Schedule C after the property you have listed from your Schedule A/B you are claiming exempt.

For example, from your Schedule A/B, you list your vehicle on your Schedule C as exempt; the specific law that would allow exemption would be either the federal exemption 11USC522(D) or your state exemption for a vehicle.

CHAPTER 14

Schedule D: Creditors Who Have Claims Secured by Property—Form B-106D

Read Schedule D carefully; if you do not have any creditors who have claims secured by property, check the first box at number 1, and go to Schedule E.

If you do have creditors who have claims against you secured by property, for example, a mortgage, car loan, judgment lien, garnishment, tax lien, mechanics lien, you check the yes box at number 1 and proceed to part 1, number 2.

In part 2, if you have a claim against you secured by property and a collection agency is now trying to collect that debt, you have to list the name of the collection agency; for example, the original creditor was Bob Martin Chevy listed in part 1, now ABC Collection Agency is trying to collect for Bob Martin Chevy; you list ABC Collection Agency in part 2 and put what line in part 1 did you list Bob Martin Chevy. If that is not your situation, put N/A in the first section of part 2, and go to Schedule E.

CHAPTER 15

Schedule E/F: Creditors Who Have Unsecured Claims—Form B106E/F

Read Schedule E/F carefully, get your three free credit reports out, and proceed to part 1. In part 1, you list any creditors who have a priority unsecured claim against you, for example, domestic support obligation from a divorce that is owed to or recoverable by a spouse or former spouse, a child support order, taxes, penalties or tickets owing to federal, state, or local governments, also anything listed in part 4, number 6A–E; if none of that applies to you, check no in number 1 in part 1, and go to part 2.

In part 2, you list any creditors who have a nonpriority unsecured claim against you. These types of creditors are listed on your credit report in the section listed as adverse accounts, including any student loans you may have and anything listed in part 4, number 6F–J.

When listing a consumer debt (AT&T), you check the box other and specify consumer debt and list the last four digits of the account number, and when was the debt incurred is listed in your credit report under date opened.

If you're married and you live in Arizona, California, Idaho, Louisiana, Nevada, New Mexico, Puerto Rico, Texas, Washington, or Wisconsin and you and your spouse are responsible for the debt, your debt is a community debt.

In part 3, you list any creditor you listed in part 2 that has placed your debt for collection if any. For example, in part 2, you would list in nonpriority unsecured creditors AT&T mobility as an original creditor, but AT&T mobility placed your debt for collection with AFNI, a collection agency.

In part 3, you would list AFNI as someone trying to collect from you for a debt you owe to AT&T Mobility. Your credit report will list the original creditor, which goes in part 2, and if the original creditor has placed your debt owed to them for collection, which would go in part 3.

In part 4, for lines 6A–D, you add up the amounts and put the total on line 6E. For lines 6F–I, you add up the amounts and put the total on line 6J.

CHAPTER 16

Schedule G: Executory Contracts and Unexpired Leases—Form B-106G

Read Schedule G carefully; if it does not apply to you, check no at number 1, and go on to Schedule H.

An example of an executory contract or unexpired lease would be you have entered into a contract to lease something like a condo, apartment, vehicle, cell phone, furniture; if that applies to you, list the appropriate information on Schedule G.

CHAPTER 17

Schedule H: Your Codebtors— Form B-106H

Read Schedule H carefully; if you and your spouse are married or you and anyone else have both signed and entered into an agreement, contract, or lease to be responsible for paying listed debt, you have a codebtor. Provide the requested information on Schedule H.

Schedule I: Your Income— Form B-106I

Read Schedule I carefully; in part 1, describe your employment status; in part 2, give the details about your monthly income; when you have completed Schedule I, go to Schedule J.

Schedule J: Your Expenses— Form B-106J

Read Schedule J carefully; in part 1, describe your household; if you're married and filing a joint case but you and your spouse live in separate households, Form B-106J will also have to be filled out. If that's not applicable, continue with your Schedule J.

In part 2, estimate your ongoing and monthly expenses.

CHAPTER 20

Declaration about an Individual Debtor's Schedules—Form B-106DEC

Read the declaration about an individual debtor's schedules carefully; if you prepared your bankruptcy forms yourself (Pro Se), check no; if you paid someone to help you prepare your bankruptcy forms, check yes, and attach Form B-119.

If you need Form B-119, bankruptcy petition preparer's notice, declaration, and signature, go to your court's website, and click the link forms, and download a copy of Form B-119.

CHAPTER 21

Summary of Your Assets and Liabilities and Certain Statistical Information—Form B-106SUM

Read the summary of your assets and liabilities and certain statistical information form carefully.

In part 1, summarize your assets; put in the totals from your Schedule A/B: Property form on lines 1A–C.

In part 2, summarize your liabilities; put in the totals from your Schedule D: Creditors Who Have Claims Secured by Property on line 2, and put in the totals from your Schedule E/F: Creditors Who Have Unsecured Priority Claims in part 1 on line 3A and a copy of the totals from part 2, nonpriority unsecured claims, on line 3B.

In part 3, summarize your income and expenses; put in the total from your Schedule I: Your Income on line 4 and the total from your Schedule J: Your Expenses on line 5.

In part 4, line 6, check yes if you are filing for bankruptcy under Chapter 7. On line 7, if your debts are primarily consumer debts, check that box. On line 8, from your Schedule I, put in the total of your current monthly income. On line 9A–F, from your Schedule E/F, put any applicable totals on the appropriate lines, and put that total on line 9G.

CHAPTER 22

Statement of Financial Affairs for Individuals Filing for Bankruptcy—Form B-107

Read the statement of financial affairs for individuals filing for bankruptcy form carefully.

In part 1, give the details about your marital status and where you lived before.

In part 2, explain your sources of income; read each question carefully; answer no if questions do not apply to you, or fill in the appropriate details if your answer is yes.

In part 3, list certain payments you made before you filed for bankruptcy; read each question carefully; answer no if questions do not apply, or fill in appropriate details if your answer is yes.

In part 4, identify legal actions, repossessions, and foreclosures; read each question carefully; answer no if questions do not apply, or fill in appropriate details if your answer is yes.

In part 5, list certain gifts and contributions; read each question carefully; answer no if questions do not apply, or fill in appropriate details if your answer is yes.

In part 6, list certain losses; read the question carefully; answer no if question does not apply, or fill in appropriate details if your answer is yes.

In part 7, list certain payments or transfers; read each question carefully; answer no if questions do not apply, or fill in appropriate details if your answer is yes.

In part 8, list certain financial accounts, instruments, safe-deposit boxes, and storage units; read each question carefully; answer no if questions do not apply, or fill in appropriate details if your answer is yes.

In part 9, identify property you hold or control for someone else; read the question carefully; answer no, or fill in appropriate details if your answer is yes.

In part 10, give details about environmental information; read each question carefully; answer no if questions do not apply, or fill in appropriate details if your answer is yes.

In part 11, give details about your business or connections to any business; read each question carefully; answer no if questions do not apply, or fill in appropriate details if your answer is yes.

In part 12, sign below, read carefully, sign, and date, and answer two questions after your signature.

CHAPTER 23

Statement About Your Social Security Numbers—Form B-121

Read the statement about your social security numbers carefully; in part 1, tell the court about yourself and your spouse, if your spouse is filing with you.

In part 2, tell the court about your social security number or numbers or with any federal individual taxpayer identification numbers you may have if any; in part 3, sign, and date.

CHAPTER 24

Chapter 7 Statement of Your Current Monthly Income—Form B-122A-1

Read the Chapter 7 statement of your current monthly income form carefully.

In part 1, calculate your current monthly income, read each question carefully, and fill in the appropriate information.

In part 2, determine whether the means test applies to you at number 12; on line 12A, copy your total current monthly income from line 11; multiply that monthly income by twelve months, and put that total on line 12B.

For example, your current monthly income is $2,000 a month; $2,000x12 months would equal to $24,000; $24,000 would go on line 12B.

In part 2, at number 13, you have to calculate the median family income that applies to you. To do that, use the chart at Appendix c.

Using the chart at Appendix c, fill in the state in which you live, fill in the number of people in your household, and then fill in the median family income for your state and size of household; put that amount in the total box for line 13.

For example, you live in the state of Alabama; there are four people in your household; using the chart at Appendix c, you would put $82,991 in the total box for line 13. If there are more than four people in your household, you would add $9,000 for each individual in excess of four.

For example, there are six people in your household; you would add $18,000 to $82,991, which equals to $100,991, and put that in the total box for line 13.

In part 2, line 14A, you have to compare line 12B, your annual income, with line 13B, the median family income, for your state. If line 12B is less than or equal to line 13, you check box 1 on the front of your Form B-122A-1; there is no presumption of abuse, sign and date your form.

For example, your annual income in line 12B is $24,000 a year; your median family income for your state and size of household (four) in line 13 is $82,991. Line 12b is less than line 13; if there is no presumption of abuse, you check box 1 on the front of your Form B-122-A1, sign, and date.

In part 2, line 14B, if your annual income at line 12B is more than in line 13, you would check box 2 on your Form B-122A-1, sign, and date, and then you would have to fill out Form B-122A-2.

For example, your annual income in line 12B is $90,000 a year; your median family income for your state and size of household (four) in line 13 is $82,991. Line 12B is more than line 13; you would check box 2 on your Form B-122A-1, sign, and date and fill out Form B-122A-2.

The information at the appendix changes periodically. If you want the most current Census Bureau's median family income by size to complete your means test, go to www.justice.gov, click on our agency, and go to alphabetical listing. Once at alphabetical listings, scroll down to US Trustee Program; click on US Trustee Program; once at US Trustee Program, click on means testing information.

Once at means testing information, scroll down to the box that says data required for completing the Form 122A and the Form 122C. From the drop-down list, pick the date you want (00/00/00) or after hit go. Once at means testing, go to Section 1. In Census Bureau's data, scroll to median family income based on state, territory, and family size, and click on that; once the chart pops up, go to your state or territory, and check your family size. If your family size is over four, add $9,000 for each in individual in excess of four.

CHAPTER 25

Statement of Exemption from Presumption of Abuse under 707(B) (2)—Form B-122A-1SUPP

If you believe that you are exempted from a presumption of abuse because you do not have primarily consumer debts or because of qualifying military service, then you would have to carefully read this form and fill in the appropriate information.

If this is not applicable to you because you primarily have consumer debts and don't have qualifying military service, you do not need to fill out this form.

CHAPTER 26

Chapter 7 Means Test Calculation—Form B-122A-2

If you filled out your Chapter 7 statement of your current monthly income, Form B-122A-1, and you checked box 2, you will need to read each question carefully on this form and fill in the appropriate information.

If you filled out your Chapter 7 statement of your current monthly income, Form B-122A-1, and you checked box 1, you do not need to fill out this form.

CHAPTER 27

Your Creditor Matrix

Now that you have completed filling out all of the necessary bankruptcy forms needed to file your Pro Se bankruptcy petition, you need to complete your creditor matrix.

A creditor matrix is a list of the names, addresses, city, state, and zip code of all your creditors. Your creditor matrix must be submitted to the clerk of the bankruptcy court online before you file your bankruptcy petition at the clerk's office. If you don't have online access, most federal courthouses in the office of the clerk of the bankruptcy court have a Pro Se clerk and also computers that Pro Se filers can use to assist them in preparing there bankruptcy forms, including completing your creditor matrix.

To find out if the clerk of the bankruptcy court in your state has a Pro Se desk and computers for Pro Se filers to use, check the court in your state in Appendix a.

To complete your creditor matrix, go to the website of the federal bankruptcy court for your state in Appendix A; once there click on the link for creditor matrix.

Once you're at the creditor matrix, it will ask for your first name, last name, email address, and phone number. You will be asked to create a password; write that password down, and don't forget it; that is the only way you will be able to get back in to review or update your creditor matrix.

Once you have created your password, you can start adding all your creditors' information—creditors' name, address, city, state, and zip code—from your Schedule D and Schedule E/F. Once you finish adding all your creditors to your creditor matrix, just click finish.

CHAPTER 28

Filing Your Bankruptcy Petition

To file your bankruptcy petition with the clerk of the bankruptcy court in your city, you should have done all of the following:

1. Completed a credit-counseling course and have a credit-counseling certificate dated within 180 days (six months) of your filing your petition
2. Have all of your bankruptcy forms filled out from Chapter 7 to Chapter 26
3. Have your creditor matrix done or ready to be done when you get to the bankruptcy clerk's office
4. Have your filing fee or filing-fee form either for a waiver or to pay the filing fee in installments filled out

If you have done all that, you are ready to file your bankruptcy petition with the bankruptcy clerk in your city and get your bankruptcy filing notice from the clerk.

CHAPTER 29

Notice of Bankruptcy Case Filing

Once your bankruptcy petition is filed with the bankruptcy clerk in your city, you will receive a "notice of bankruptcy case filing" receipt from the clerk's office. This notice will have your bankruptcy case number, date, and time your bankruptcy petition was filed.

Your "notice of bankruptcy case filing" will notify creditors that the filing of your bankruptcy case automatically stays certain collection and other actions against you. Also, if the creditor attempts to collect a debt, they could be penalized. If you have an emergency situation such as getting utilities turned back on, stopping an eviction for at least thirty days, having a driver's license reinstated if suspended for failure to pay citations, or creditors calling, emailing, or texting, you can call them; ask for their fax, text, or email number/address; and provide them a copy of your "notice of bankruptcy case filing" or give them your case number.

By giving your "notice of bankruptcy case filing" case number and/or a copy of that notice to your utility provider, you should have your utility services cut back on the same day or the next day. If your services have not been disconnected yet, your services should remain on, and you should be given a new account number.

If you're facing eviction and have taken the steps at Chapter 8 and Chapter 9, you should be able to avoid an eviction for at least thirty days or put a foreclosure or repossession on hold. If your driver's license is suspended for only failure to pay tickets, the Department of

Motor Vehicles (DMV) should reinstate your driver's license, which would also allow you to reestablish payment plans with the municipality, without standing tickets against you, and if creditors have been calling, emailing, or texting you, they must stop immediately.

CHAPTER 30

Meeting of Creditors

Shortly after you file your bankruptcy petition and receive your "notice of bankruptcy case filing," you'll receive a notice in the mail informing you of the date you must attend the meeting of creditors. The meeting of creditors is a meeting between you, your creditors, and a bankruptcy trustee.

The meeting of creditors is an opportunity for any of your creditors to object to the discharge of the debt you owe them. During the meeting of creditors, the bankruptcy trustee will ask you some questions about your bankruptcy petition and verify your identity. The notice of meeting of creditors will tell you valid photo identification is required (driver's license) and proof of social security number (social security card) is required.

If you filed jointly, both parties have to bring those items, and both of you have to attend the meeting of creditors.

You must attend the meeting of creditors; if you do not attend, your bankruptcy petition will be dismissed, your debts will no longer be stayed, and you will not receive a discharge of any of your debts.

CHAPTER 31

Certification about a Financial Management Course—Form B-423

The second course you must take to obtain a discharge in your bankruptcy case is the "personal financial management course."

If you have not already taken this course and filed your certificate of completion for the "personal financial management course" before the meeting of creditors, you should do so no later than after you attend the meeting of creditors.

Failure to take the "personal financial management course" and file that certificate with the bankruptcy court or the certification about a financial management course (Form B-423) will result in your case being closed, without discharge of any of your debts.

CHAPTER 32

Conclusion

If you have gotten your credit-counseling certificate filed along with your bankruptcy petition, paid your filing fee in full, attended your meeting of creditors, and filed your certification about a financial management course with the court, all you have to do is wait for the order from the bankruptcy court discharging all your dischargeable debts.

You will receive an order of discharge, which will explain the bankruptcy discharge in your Chapter 7 case.

I hope you enjoyed using what you learned from *How to File Your Own Bankruptcy* and that as a result, you are able to overcome your financial hardships and enjoy a healthier, happier, and more debt-free life.

US Bankruptcy Court Information

US Bankruptcy Court/Southern District of Alabama
www.alnb.uscourts.gov
Robert S. Vance Federal Building
1800 Fifth Avenue North
Birmingham, Alabama 35203
Telephone: (205) 714-4000
Fax: (205) 909-9432
Northern Division
400 Well Street
Decatur, Alabama 35601
Telephone: (256) 584-7900
Fax: (256) 584-7977
Western Division
2005 University Boulevard
Tuscaloosa, Alabama 35401
Telephone: (205) 561-1600
Fax: (205) 561-1640
Eastern Division
1129 Noble Street
Anniston, Alabama 36201
Telephone: (256) 741-1500
Fax: (256) 741-1521

District of Alaska US Bankruptcy Court
www.akb.uscourts.gov
Anchorage
605 W. 4th Ave. Suite 138
Anchorage, AK 99501
Telephone: (907) 271-2655
Toll-Free: (800) 859-8059
Fairbanks
101 12th Ave. Room 332
Fairbanks, AK 99701
Telephone: (907) 456-0349
Toll-Free: (866) 243-3813

Note: Whatever district serves your city is where you file your bankruptcy petition. The court's website may give you that information, or you can call the clerk's office.

District of Arizona US Bankruptcy Court
www.azb.uscourts.gov
US Courthouse and Federal Building
230 North 1st Avenue Suite 101
Phoenix, AZ 85003
Telephone: (602) 682-4000 or (800) 556-9230
Tucson
James A. Walsh Federal Courthouse
38 South Scott Avenue Ste 100
Tucson, AZ 85701
Telephone: (502) 202-7500 or (800) 556-9230
Yuma
John M. Roll US Courthouse
98 West 1st Street 2nd Floor
Yuma, AZ 85364
Telephone: (928) 261-4500 or (800) 556-9230

US Bankruptcy Court for the Eastern and Western Districts of Arkansas
www.arb.uscourts.gov
Little Rock
US Bankruptcy Court
300 W. 2nd Street
Little Rock, AR 72201
Telephone: (501) 918-5500
Fayetteville
US Bankruptcy Court
35 E. Mountain Street Room 316
Fayetteville, AR 72701
Telephone: (479) 582-9800

US Bankruptcy Court California
www.cacb.uscourts.gov
US Bankruptcy Court
255 E Temple St.
Los Angeles, CA 90012
Telephone: (855) 460-9641
US Bankruptcy Court
450 Golden Gate Ave. Ste 36099
San Francisco, CA 94102
Telephone: (415) 268-2300
US Bankruptcy Court
1300 Clay Street Suite 300
Oakland, CA 94612
Telephone: (510) 879-3600
Bankruptcy Court
21041 Burbank Blvd Ste 1
Woodland Hills, CA 91367
Telephone: (818) 587-2840

US Bankruptcy Court Colorado
   www.cob.uscourts.gov
   72119th St
   Denver, CO 80202
   Telephone: (720) 904-7300

US Bankruptcy Court for the District of Connecticut
   www.ctb.uscqurts.gov
   US Bankruptcy Court
   Abraham Ribicoff Federal Building
   450 Main Street 7th Floor
   Hartford, CT 06103
   Telephone: (860) 240-3675 or (860) 240-3679
   US Bankruptcy Court
   Brien McMahon Federal Building
   915 Lafayette Boulevard
   Bridgeport, CT 06604
   US Bankruptcy Court
   Connecticut Financial Center
   157 Church Street 18th Fl
   New Haven, CT 06510
   Telephone: (203) 773-2009

District of Delaware US Bankruptcy Court
   www.ded.uscourtss.gov
   824 N Market St. 3rd FL
   Wilmington, DE 19801
   Telephone: (302) 252-2900

District of Columbia US Bankruptcy Court
   www.dcd.uscourts.gov
   333 Constitution Ave. NW
   Washington, DC 20001
   Telephone: (202) 354-3280 40

US Bankruptcy Court Florida
www.flsb.uscourts.gov
US Bankruptcy Court
801 N Florida Ave Ste 700
Tampa, FL 33602
Telephone: (813) 301-5162
C. Clyde Atkins US Courthouse
301 North Miami Avenue Rm 150
Telephone: (305) 714-1800
US Bankruptcy Court
1515 North Flagler Drive Suite 801
West Palm Beach, FL 33401
Telephone: (561) 514-4100
US Courthouse
299 East Broward Blvd. Room 112
Fort Lauderdale, FL 33301
Telephone: (954) 769-5700

US Bankruptcy Court Georgia
www.ganb.uscourts.gov
US Bankruptcy Court
600 James Brown Blvd
Augusta, GA 30901
Telephone: (706) 724-2421
US Bankruptcy Court
75 Ted Turner Dr. SW
Atlanta, GA 30303
Telephone: (404) 215-1000
US Bankruptcy Court
121 Spring St. Se
Gainesville, GA 30501
Telephone: (676) 450-2700

US Bankruptcy Court District of Hawaii
www.hib.uscourts.gov
US Bankruptcy Court

1132 Bishop St.
Honolulu, HI 96813
Telephone: (808) 522-8100

US Bankruptcy Court Idaho
www.id.uscourt.gov
US Bankruptcy Court
550 W Fort St Ste 400
Boise, ID 83724
Telephone: (208) 334-1361
US Bankruptcy Court
6450 Mineral Dr. Ste 150
Coeur D Alene, ID 83815
Telephone: (208) 665-6850
US Bankruptcy Court
801 E Sherman St. Rm 119
Pocatello, ID 83201
Telephone: (208) 478-4123

US Bankruptcy Court Illinois
www.ilnb.uscourts.gov
US Bankruptcy Court
Eastern Division
219 S Dearborn
Chicago, IL 60604
Telephone: (312) 408 5000
US Bankruptcy Court
Western Division
327 South Church Street
Rockford, IL 61101
Telephone: (815) 987-4350
US Bankruptcy Court
750 Missouri Ave
East Saint Louis, IL 62201
Telephone: (618) 482-9400
US Bankruptcy Court

100 N.E. Monroe St. Ste 216
Peoria, IL 61602
Telephone: (309) 671-7035

US Bankruptcy Court Indiana
www.innb.uscourts.gov
US Bankruptcy Court
46 E Ohio St Ste 116
Indianapolis, IN 46204
Telephone: (317) 229-3800
US Bankruptcy Court
401 South Michigan Street
South Bend, IN 46601
Telephone: (574) 968-2100
US Bankruptcy Court
1300 S. Harrison St. Ste 1188
Fort Wayne, IN 46802
Telephone: (260) 420-5100
US Bankruptcy Court
5400 Federal Plaza Ste 3600
Hammond, IN 46320
Telephone: (219) 852-3480

US Bankruptcy Court Iowa
www.iasb.uscourts.gov
US Bankruptcy Court
110 E Court Ave Ste 300
Des Moines, IA 50309
Telephone: (515) 284-6230
US Bankruptcy Court
111 Seventh Avenue Se Ste 15
Cedar Rapids, IA 52401
Telephone: (319) 286-2200
US Bankruptcy Court
320 6th Street Rm 126
Sioux City, IA 51101

District Of Kansas/US Bankruptcy Court
   www.ksb.uscourts.gov
   Robert J Dole Courthouse
   500 State Avenue Rm 161
   Kansas City, KS 66101
   Telephone: (913) 735-2110
   Wichita US Bankruptcy Court
   US Courthouse
   401 N Market Rm 107
   Wichita, KS 67202
   Telephone: (316) 315-4150
   Topeka US Bankruptcy Court
   Frank Carlson Federal Building
   444 Se Quincy Rm 240
   Topeka, KS 66683
   Telephone: (785) 295-2611

US Bankruptcy Court Kentucky
   www.kyeb.uscourts.gov
   US Bankruptcy Court
   601 W Broadway Ste 450
   Louisville, KY 40202
   Telephone: (859) 233-2608
   US Bankruptcy Court Clerk's Office
   All Divisions
   Telephone: (859) 233-2608

US Bankruptcy Court Louisiana
   www.laeb.uscourts.gov
   US Bankruptcy Court
   707 Florida St Rm 119
   Baton Rouge, LA 70801
   Telephone: (225) 346-3333
   US Bankruptcy Court
   500 Poydras Street Suite B-601
   New Orleans, LA 70130

Telephone: (504) 589-7878
US Courthouse
300 Jackson Street Suite 116
Alexandria, LA 71301
Telephone: (318) 445-1890 or (866) 356-5221
US Courthouse
611 Broad Street 1st Floor
Lake Charles, LA 70501
Telephone: (337) 262-6800 or (866) 789-6015
US Courthouse
201 Jackson Street
Monroe, LA 71201
Shreveport
US Courthouse
300 Fannin Street Suite 2201
Shreveport, LA 71101
Telephone: (318) 676-4267 or (866) 721-2105

District of Maine US Bankruptcy Court
www.meb.uscourts.gov
US Bankruptcy Court
District of Maine
537 Congress Street 2nd Floor
Portland, ME 04101
Telephone: (207) 780-3482
US Bankruptcy Court
Mc Smith Federal Building
202 Harlow Street 3rd Floor
Bangor, ME 04401
Telephone: (207) 945-0348

US Bankruptcy Court Maryland
www.mdb.uscourts.gov
US Bankruptcy Court
101 W Lombard St.
Baltimore, MD 21201

Telephone: (410) 962-2688
US Bankruptcy Court
6500 Cherrywood Ln
Greenbelt, MD 20770
Telephone: (301) 344-8018

District of Massachusetts US Bankruptcy Court
www.mab.uscourts.gov
US Bankruptcy Court
John McCormack
5 Post Office Square Suite 1150
Boston, MA 02109
Telephone: (617) 748-5300
Fax: (617) 748-5315
US Bankruptcy Court
Donohue Federal Building
595 Main Street Rm 311
Worcester, MA 01608
Telephone: (508) 770-8900
Fax: (508) 770-8975
US Bankruptcy Court
300 State Street
Springfield, MA 01105
Telephone: (413) 785-6900
Fax: (413) 781-9477

US Bankruptcy Court Michigan
www.mieb.uscourts.gov
Bay City
111 First Street
Bay City, Michigan 48708
Telephone: (989) 894-8840
Detroit
211 West Fort Street
Detroit, Michigan 48226
Telephone: (313) 234-0065

Flint
226 West Second Street
Flint, Michigan 48502
Telephone: (810) 235-4126

District of Minnesota US Bankruptcy Court
www.mnb.uscourts.gov
200 Warren E Burger Federal Building
316 North Robert Street
St. Paul, MN 55101
Telephone: (651) 848-1000
301 Diana E. Murphy US Courthouse
300 South Fourth Street
Minneapolis, MN 55415
Telephone: (612) 664-5200 or (866) 260-7337
404 Gerald W. Heaney Federal Building
515 West First Street
Duluth, MN 55802
Telephone: (218) 529-3600

US Bankruptcy Court Mississippi
www.msnb.uscourts.gov
501 E Court St Ste 2300
Jackson, MS 39201
Telephone: (601) 608-4600
2012 15th St. Ste 244
Gulfport, MS 39501
Telephone: (228) 563-1790

US Bankruptcy Court Missouri
www.moeb.uscourts.gov
Thomas F. Eagleton US Courthouse
111 South 10th St.4th Floor
St. Louis, MO 63102
Telephone: (314) 244-4500
Rush Hudson Limbaugh Sr. US Courthouse

5555 Independence St.
Cape Girardeau, MO 63703
US Bankruptcy Court
400 E 9th St. #1510a
Kansas City, MO 64106

US Bankruptcy Court Montana
www.mtb.uscourts.gov
Mike Mansfield Federal Courthouse
400 North Main Street 2nd Floor
Butte, MT 59701
Telephone: (406) 497-1240 or (888) 888-2530
James F. Battin Federal Courthouse
2601 2nd Avenue North
Billings, MT 59101
Telephone: (406) 247-7000
Fax: (406) 247-7008
Missouri River Federal Courthouse
125 Central Avenue West
Great Falls, MT 59404
Telephone: (406) 727-1922
Fax: (406) 727-7648
Russell Smith Federal Courthouse
201 E Broadway
Missoula, MT 59802
Telephone: (406) 542-7260
Fax: (406) 542-7272

District of Nebraska US Bankruptcy Court
www.neb.uscourts.gov
Roman L. Hruska US Courthouse
111 South 18th Plaza Suite 1125
Omaha, NE 68102
Telephone: (402) 661-7444
460 Robert Denney Federal Building
US Courthouse

100 Centennial Mall North
Lincoln, NE 68508
Telephone: (402) 437-1625

US Bankruptcy Court Nevada
www.nvb.uscourts.gov
Foley Federal Building
300 Las Vegas Blvd. South
Las Vegas, NV 89101
Telephone: (702) 527-7000
C. Clifton Young Federal Building
300 Booth Street
Reno, NV 89509
Telephone: (775) 326-2100

District of New Hampshire US Bankruptcy Court
www.nhb.uscourts.gov
Warren B. Rudman US Courthouse
55 Pleasant Street Room 200
Concord, NH 03301
Telephone: (603) 222-2600

US Bankruptcy Court New Jersey
www.njb.uscourts.gov
Martin Luther King Jr. Federal Building
50 Walnut Street
Newark, NJ 07102
Telephone: (973) 645-4764
Clarkson S. Fisher US Courthouse
402 East State Street
Trenton, NJ 08608
Telephone: (609) 858-9333
US Post Office and Courthouse
401 Market Street
Camden, NJ 08101
Telephone: (856) 361-2300

District of New Mexico US Bankruptcy Court
    www.nmb.uscourts.gov
    Pete V. Domenici US Courthouse
    333 Lomas Blvd. NW Suite 360
    Albuquerque, NM 87102
    Telephone: (505) 415-7999 or (866) 291-6805 Toll-Free

US Bankruptcy Court New York
    www.nysb.uscourts.gov
    US Bankruptcy Court
    One Bowling Green
    New York, NY 10004
    Telephone: (212) 688-2870
    US Bankruptcy Court
    355 Main Street
    Poughkeepsie, NY 12601
    Telephone: (845) 451-6372
    US Bankruptcy Court
    300 Quarropas Street Room 248
    White Plains, NY 10601
    Telephone: (914) 467-7250

US Bankruptcy Court North Carolina
    www.nceb.uscourts.gov
    US Bankruptcy Court
    Century Station Federal Building
    300 Fayetteville St 4th FL
    Raleigh, NC 27601
    Telephone: (919) 856-4752
    US Bankruptcy Court
    Randy D. Doub Courthouse
    150 Reade Circle
    Greenville, NC 27858
    Telephone: (919) 856-4752
    US Bankruptcy Court
    1003 S. 17th Street Room 118

Wilmington, NC 28401
US Bankruptcy Court
3rd Floor 301 Green Street
Fayetteville, NC 28302

US Bankruptcy Court North Dakota
www.ndb.uscourts.gov
Quentin N. Burdick US Courthouse
655 1st Ave North Suite 210
Fargo, ND 58102
Telephone: (701) 297-?

US Bankruptcy Court Ohio
www.ohnb.uscqurts.ghov
John F. Seiberling Federal Building
455 US Courthouse
2 South Main Street
Akron, Ohio 44308
Telephone: (330) 252-6100
Fax: (330) 252-6115
Ralph Regula Federal Building
401 Mckinley Avenue SW
Canton, Ohio 44702
Telephone: (330) 458-2120
Fax: (330) 458-2451
Howard M. Metzenbaum US Courthouse
201 Superior Avenue
Cleveland, Ohio 44114
Telephone: (216) 615-4300
Fax: (216) 615-4363
James M. Ashley and Thomas W.L. Ashley
US Courthouse
1716 Spielbusch Avenue
Toledo, Ohio 43604
Telephone: (419) 213-5600
Fax: (419) 213-5650

Nathaniel R. Jones Federal Building
10 East Commerce Street
Youngstown, Ohio 44503
Telephone: (330) 742-0900
Fax: (330) 742-0902

US Bankruptcy Court Oklahoma
www.okwb.uscourts.gov
US Bankruptcy Court
215 Dean A. Mcgee Ave. Ste 147
Oklahoma City, OK 73102
Telephone: (405) 609-5700
US Bankruptcy Court
224 S. Boulder Ave. Ste 105
Tulsa, OK 74103
Telephone: (918) 699-4000

US Bankruptcy Court Oregon
www.orb.uscourts.gov
US Bankruptcy Court
1050 SW 6th Ave #700
Portland, OR 97204
Telephone: (503) 326-1500

US Bankruptcy Court Pennsylvania
www.paeb.uscourts.gov
US Bankruptcy Court
600 Grant St.
Pittsburgh, PA 152319
Telephone: (412) 644 2700
US Bankruptcy Court
900 Market St.
Philadelphia, PA 19107
Telephone: (215) 408-2800
US Bankruptcy Court
17 S Park Row

Erie, PA 16501
Telephone: (814) 464-9740
US Bankruptcy Court
228 Walnut St. Ste 320
Harrisburg, PA 17101
Telephone: (717) 901-2800

US Bankruptcy Court District of Rhode Island
www.rib.uscourts.gov
US Bankruptcy Court
380 Westminster St. Ste 6
Providence, RI 02903
Telephone: (401) 626-3100

US Bankruptcy Court South Carolina
www.scb.uscourts.gov
US Bankruptcy Court
King and Queen Building
145 King Street Room 225
Charleston, SC 29401
Telephone: (803) 765-5436
US Bankruptcy Court
1100 Laurel St.
Columbia, SC 29201
Telephone: (803) 765-5436

US Bankruptcy Court District of South Dakota
www.sdb.uscourts.gov
US Bankruptcy Court
225 South Pierce Street Room 203
Pierre, SD 57501
Telephone: (605) 945-4460
US Bankruptcy Court
400 South Phillips Avenue Room 104
Sioux Falls, SD 57104
Telephone: (605) 357-2400

US Bankruptcy Court Tennessee
  www.tnmb.uscourts.gov
  US Bankruptcy Court
  Middle District of Tennessee
  701 Broadway Room 170
  Nashville, TN 37203
  Telephone: (615) 736-5584
  US Bankruptcy Court
  31 East 11th Street
  Chattanooga, TN 37402
  Telephone: (423) 752-5163
  US Bankruptcy Court
  220 West Depot Street Suite 218
  Greenville, TN 37743
  Telephone: (423) 787-0113
  US Bankruptcy Court
  800 Market Street Suite 330
  Knoxville, TN 37902
  Telephone: (865) 545-4279
  US Bankruptcy Court
  Second Floor Courtroom
  200 South Jefferson Street
  Winchester, TN 37398
  Telephone: (423) 752-5163

US Bankruptcy Court Texas
  www.txnb.uscourts.gov
  US Bankruptcy Court
  George Mahon Federal Building
  1205 Texas Ave. Rm 306
  Lubbock, TX 79401
  Telephone: (806) 472-5000
  US Bankruptcy Court
  J Marvin Jones Federal Building
  205 Southeast Fifth Ave Rm 2010
  Amarillo, TX 79101

Telephone: (806) 324-2302
US Bankruptcy Court
Earle Cabell Federal Building
1100 Commerce St. Rm 1254
Dallas, TX 75242
Telephone: (214) 753-2000
US Bankruptcy Court
Eldon B. Mahon US Courthouse
501 W. 10th St
Fort Worth, TX 76102
Telephone: (817) 333-6000

US Bankruptcy Court District of Utah
www.utb.uscourts.gov
US Bankruptcy Court
Frank E. Moss US Courthouse
350 South Main Street 3rd Floor
Salt Lake City, Utah 84101
Telephone: (801) 524-2013

US Bankruptcy Court District of Vermont
www.vtb.uscourts.gov
US Bankruptcy Court Federal Building
11 Elmwood Ave. Rm 240
Burlington, VT 05401
Telephone: (802) 657-6400
Toll-Free: (844) 644-7459
US Bankruptcy Court District of Vermont
151 West Street
Rutland, VT 05701
Telephone: (802) 657-6400
Toll-Free: (844) 644-7459

US Bankruptcy Court District of Virginia
www.vaeb.uscourts.gov
US Bankruptcy Court

200 S. Washington St
Alexandria, VA 22314
Telephone: (703) 258-1200
US Bankruptcy Court 600
Granby Street 4th Floor
Norfolk, VA 23510
Telephone: (757) 222-7500
US Bankruptcy Court
701 East Broad Street Suite 4000
Richmond, VA 23219
Telephone: (804) 916-2400
US Bankruptcy Court
2400 West Avenue
Newport News, VA 23607
Telephone: (757) 222-7500

US Bankruptcy Court Washington
www.wawb.uscourts.gov
US Bankruptcy Court
700 Stewart St. #6301
Seattle, WA 98101
Telephone: (206) 370-5200
US Bankruptcy Court
Union Station
1717 Pacific Avenue Ste 2100
Tacoma, WA 98402
Telephone: (253) 882-3900
US Bankruptcy Court
Federal Building
500 W 12th 2nd Floor
Vancouver, WA 98660

US Bankruptcy Court
Kitsap County Courthouse
614 Division St
Port Orchard, WA 98366

US Bankruptcy Court
Everett Station
Weyerhaeuser Room 4th Floor
3201 South Avenue
Everett, WA 98201

US Bankruptcy Court West Virginia
www.wvnb.uscourts.gov
US Bankruptcy Court
1125 Chapline Street
Wheeling, WV 26003
Telephone: (304) 233-1655
US Bankruptcy Court
324 West Main Street
Clarksburg, WV 26301
Telephone: (304) 233-1655
US Bankruptcy Court
300 Virginia St. E Ste 3200
Charleston, WV 25301
Telephone: (304) 347-3003

US Bankruptcy Court Wisconsin
www.wieb.uscourts.gov
US Bankruptcy Court
517 East Wisconsin Avenue Room 126
Milwaukee, WI 53202
Telephone: (414) 297-3291
US Bankruptcy Court
Western District of Wisconsin
120 North Henry Street Room 340
Madison, WI 53703
Telephone: (608) 264-5178

US Bankruptcy Court District of Wyoming
www.wyb.uscourts.gov
US Bankruptcy Court

District of Wyoming
2120 Capitol Avenue 6th Floor
Cheyenne, WY 82001
Telephone: (307) 433-2200
US Bankruptcy Court
District of Wyoming
111 South Wolcott
Casper, WY 82601
Telephone: (307) 433-2200
Commonwealth or US Territory

US Bankruptcy Court District of Guam
www.gud.uscourts.gov
District Court of Guam
520 W Soledad Ave Floor 4
Hagatna, Guam 96910
Telephone: (671) 969-4500
Fax: (671) 969-4488

US Bankruptcy Court for the Northern Mariana Islands
www.nmid.uscourts.gov
US District Court for the Northern Mariana Islands
2nd Floor Horiguchi Building
123 Kopa Di Oru Street
Beach Road Garapan
Saipan, MP 96950
Telephone: 1-(670) 237-1200

US Bankruptcy Court District of Puerto Rico
www.prb.uscourts.gov
Jose V. Toledo Federal Building & US Courthouse
300 Recinto Sur Street
San Juan, PR 00901
Telephone: (787) 977-6000

MCS Building Suite 222A
800 Tito Castro Avenue
Ponce, PR 00716

US Bankruptcy Court for the US Virgin Islands
www.vid.uscourts.gov
Federal Building on St. Thomas
5500 Veterans Dr. Room 310
St. Thomas, VI 00802
Telephone: (340) 774-8310
Fax: (340) 775-8076

Federal/State Exemptions

EXEMPTIONS

An exemption is a law that allows you to keep certain property. In some states, you can choose to use either the state exemptions or the federal exemptions; you may not mix and match federal and state exemptions. You must pick one or the other.

For each thing that you own that you have listed on either Schedule A/B, you must list those on Schedule C and claim exempt. If you do not claim the exempt, the trustee may take the property and sell it and pay your creditors.

Some exemption amounts may double if you are married.

What is equity? If you own a car, it is worth $5,000, but you took a loan out on the car, and there is a lien on the car in the amount of $4,000; you have $1,000 in equity ($5,000 value minus $4,000 left to pay on the loan equals $1,000).

If the total amount of all your property is less than $13,000, you can exempt all your property under 522 (d)(5)

Household goods means:

- Clothing
- Furniture
- Appliances
- One radio
- One television
- One VCR
- Linens
- China
- Crockery
- Kitchenware

Educational materials and educational equipment primarily for the use of minor dependent children of the debtor.

Medical equipment and supplies

Furniture exclusively for the use of minor children or elderly or disabled dependents of the debtor.

Personal effects (including the toys and hobby equipment of minor dependent children and wedding rings) of debtor and the dependents of the debtor.

One personal computer and related equipment.

FEDERAL EXEMPTIONS

Household goods and clothing	11USC522(d) (3) $12,625 (no item over $600)
Jewelry	11USC522(d) (4) $1,600
Tools of trade (business assets)	11USC522(d) (6) $2,375
Life insurance policies (cash value)	11USC522(d) (8) $12,625
Personal injury	11USC522(d) (11) (d) $23,675
Retirement benefits (pensions, 401(k)/(m), IRA)	11USC522(d) (10) (A)©
Equity in car/motor vehicle	11USC522(d) (2) $3,775
Homestead (equity in your home)	11USC522(d) (1) $23,675
Wild card (assets not listed above)	11USC522(d) (5) $1,250+$11,850 of any unused amount of the exemption under subsection (d) (1)

State Exemptions

Alabama	No federal exemptions allowed
Homestead	Ala. Code 6-10-2
	$5,000
Car	100 percent for business
Personal property	Ala. Code 6-10-5; 6-10-6
	Unlimited
Wild card	Ala. Code 6-10-6
	$3,000
Alaska	Federal exemptions allowed
Homestead	$70,200
Car	$3,900
Personal property	$3,900
Tools of trade	$2,800
Wild card	None
	No federal exemptions allowed
Arizona	Arizona code
	ARS 33-1101
Homestead	$150,000
	ARS 33-1125 (8)
Car	$6,000
	ARS 33-1123; 1124; 1125 (1)-(8)
Personal property	$6,000
	ARS 33-1126(A) (1)
Life insurance	$20,000
	ARS 33-1130(1)
Tools of trade	$5,000
	None
Wild card	

Arkansas	Federal exemptions allowed
	State statutes/constitution
Homestead	9-3, 9-4, 9-5; 16-66-210, 16-66-218(A)(1), 16-66-218(B)(3)(4)
	Unlimited
Car	16-66-218(A)(2)
	$1,200
Personal property	16-66-218(A)(1)
Tools of trade	16-66-218(A)(4)
	$750
Wild card	9-1, 9-2; 16-66-218(B)(1)(2)
	$500 of any personal property if married or head of family, else $200
California	No federal exemptions allowed
	Calif. Stat. 704 or 703
Homestead	704.710, 704.720, 704.730
	$75,000
Car	704.010
Personal property	704.020; 704.080; 704.030; 704.200; 704.050; 704.040
Life insurance	704.100(B)
Tools of trade	704.060
Wild card	None
Homestead	703.140(B)(1)
	703.140(B)(2)
Car	$2,775
	703.140(B)(3); 703.140(B)(9);
Personal property	703.140(B)(4)
Life insurance	703.140(B)(1)(C); 703.140(B)(8)
Tools of trade	703.140(B)(6)
Wild card	703.140(B)(5)

Colorado

Homestead

Car

Personal property
Life insurance
Tools of trade
Wild card

Connecticut

Homestead

Car
Personal property
Life insurance
Tools of trade
Wild card

Delaware

Homestead
Car
Personal property
Life insurance
Tools of trade
Wild card

No federal exemptions allowed
Colorado code
CRS 38-41-201; 38-4-201.6; 38-41-203; 38-41-207
$60,000
13-54-102(J)(1)(11)
$3,000
13-54-102(1)(A)-(P)
10-7-106; 13-54-102(1)(1)(B); 13-54-102(1)(1)(A)
13-54-102(1)(G); 13-54-102(1)(i)(K)
None

Federal exemptions allowed
Connecticut code
52-352b(CT)
$75,000
52-352b(j)
52-352b(a);(c);(f);(i);(k);(l);(q)
52-352b(s)
52-352b(1);(b)
52-352b(r)
$1,000

No federal exemptions allowed
Delaware code
$125,000
10-4914
10-4902(A);(C);(D)
18-2729; 18-2725
10-4902(b)
10-4903

District of Columbia	Federal exemptions allowed DC code
Homestead	15-501(A)(14) Unlimited
Car	15-501(A)(1) $2,575
Personal property	15-501(A)(2) $8,625
Life insurance	15-501(A)(5)
Tools of trade	15-501(A)(4) $1,625
Wild card	15-501(A)(3) $8,075
Florida	No federal exemptions allowed Florida code
Homestead	222.01; 222.02; 222.03; 222.05
Car	222.25 $1,000
Personal property	222.25 $1,000
Life insurance	222.14
Tools of trade	None
Wild card	$1,000
Georgia	No federal exemptions allowed Georgia code
Homestead	44-13-100(A)(1)
Car	44-13-100(A)(3)
Personal property	44-13-100(A)(1)-(A)(11)
Life insurance	44-13-100(A)(8);(9);(11)(C)
Tools of trade	44-13-100(A)(7) $500
Wild card	44-13-100(A)(1);(6)

Hawaii	Federal exemptions allowed
	Hawaii code
Homestead	36-651-91; 36-651-92; 36-651-96
	$20,000
Car	36-651-12(2)
	$2,575
Personal property	36-651-12(1);(2);(4);(5)
Life insurance	24-431:10-D:112
Tools of trade	36-651-121(3)
Wild card	None
Idaho	No federal exemptions allowed
	Idaho code
	55-1003
Homestead	$100,000
	11-605(3)
Car	11-605
Personal property	$750 per item—$7,500 total
	11-605(10)
Wild card	$800
	No federal exemptions allowed
Illinois	Illinois code
	735-5/12-901; 906
Homestead	$15,000
	735-5/12-1001(C)
Car	$2,400
	735-5/12-1001 (A)-(G)
Personal property	215-5/238;735-5/12-1001 (F)
Life insurance	735-5/12-1001(D)
	$1,500
Tools of trade	735-5/12-1001(B)
	$4,000
Wild card	

Indiana	No federal exemptions allowed
	Indiana code
Homestead	34-55-10(2)(B)(1);(C);34-55-10 2(B)(5)
Car	$17,600
Personal property	None
Life insurance	34-2-28-1 (A)(3);(4)
Tools of trade	27-1-12-14; 27-2-5-1
Wild card	10-2-6-3
	34-55-10-2(B)(2)
	$4,000

Iowa	No federal exemptions allowed
	Iowa code
	499A.18; 561.2; 561.16; 561.4
Homestead	627.6(9)
Car	627.6(1)-(9)
Personal property	627.6(6)
Life insurance	627.6(11)
Tools of trade	627.6(13)
Wild card	

Kansas	No federal exemptions allowed
	Kansas code
	60-2301
Homestead	Unlimited
	60-2304(C)
Car	To $20,000
	60-2304(A)-(E)
Personal property	40-414(B); 60-2313(A)(7)
Life insurance	None
Wild card	

Kentucky	Federal exemptions allowed
	Kentucky code
Homestead	427.060; 427.090
	$5,000
Car	427.010(1)
	$2,500
Personal property	427.010(1)
	$3,000
	304.14-340; 304.14-350; 304.14-300
Life insurance	427.040
Tools of trade	$1,000
	427.160
Wild card	$1,000
Louisiana	No federal exemptions allowed
	Louisiana code
Homestead	20:1
	$35,000
Personal property	13:3881A(4);(5)
Life insurance	22:647
Tools of trade	13:3881A(2)
Wild card	None
Maine	No federal exemptions allowed
	Maine code
Homestead	14-4422(1)
	$47,500
	14-4422(2)
Car	14-4422(2)-(14)
Personal property	14-4422(10);(11)
Life insurance	14-4422(5);(8);(9)
Tools of trade	14-4422(15)
Wild card	$400

Maryland	No federal exemptions allowed
	Maryland code
Homestead	11-504
	$22,975
Personal property	11-504(B)(2);(3);(4)
Life insurance	INS 16-11(A)
Tools of trade	11-504(B)(1)
	$5,000
Wild card	11-504(B)(5)(F)
	$6,000 of cash or property of any kind
Massachusetts	Federal exemptions allowed
	Mass. code
	188.1; 188-1A
Homestead	235-34
Personal property	175-119A; 175-125
Life insurance	235-34
Tools of trade	None
Wild card	
Michigan	Federal exemptions allowed
	Michigan code
Homestead	600.5451(1)(M);(N)
	$30,000
Car	600.5454(1)(G)
	$2,775
Personal property	600.5454(1)(A)-(H)
Tools of trade	600.5451(1)(I)
Wild card	None
Minnesota	Federal exemptions allowed
	Minnesota code
Homestead	510.02
Car	550.37
Personal property	550.37
Tools of trade	550.37
Wild card	None

Mississippi	No federal exemptions allowed
	Mississippi code
Homestead	85-3-21
	$75,000
Car	None
	85-3-1 (A)
Personal property	$10,000
	None
Life insurance	85-3-1 (A)
Tools of trade	85-3-1 (A)
Wild card	
Missouri	No federal exemptions allowed
	Missouri code
Homestead	513.475
Car	513.430
Personal property	513.430(1)-(9)
Life insurance	376.530; 376.550; 513.430(7)
Tools of trade	513.430(4)
Wild card	513.430(3); 513.440
Montana	No federal exemptions allowed
	Montana code
	70-32-104
Homestead	$250,000
	25-13-608(1)(A)
Car	25-13-609(1)
Personal property	80-2-245
Life insurance	25-13-609(3); 25-13-613(B)
Tools of trade	None
Wild card	
Nebraska	No federal exemptions allowed
	Nebraska code
	40-101-108
Homestead	$60,000
	None
Car	25-1556
Personal property	44-371
Life insurance	25-1552
Tools of trade	25-1552
Wild card	

Nevada	No federal exemptions allowed
	Nevada code
Homestead	21.090(1)(L)
	$550,000
Car	21.090(1)(F);(O)
Personal property	21.090(1)(A)-(P)
Life insurance	21.090(1)(K);687B.260
Tools of trade	21.090(1)(C);(D);(E);(i)
Wild card	None
New Hampshire	Federal exemptions allowed
	New Hampshire code
Homestead	480:1
	$100,000
Car	511:2(XVI)
	$4,000
Personal property	511:2(I)-(XVII)
Life insurance	None
Tools of trade	511:2(VII);(IX);(XII)
Wild card	None
New Jersey	Federal exemptions allowed
	New Jersey code
Homestead	None
Car	None
Personal property	2a:17-19; 2a:26-4
	$1,000
Life insurance	17b:24-10; 17b:24-6b
Tools of trade	None
Wild card	None

New Mexico	Federal exemptions allowed
	New Mexico code
Homestead	42-10-0
	$60,000
Car	42-10-1; 42-10-2
	$4,000
Personal property	42-10-1; 42-10-2; 48-2-15; 70-4-12
	42-10-3
Life insurance	42-10-1; 42-10-2
Tools of trade	42-10-10
Wild card	

New York	Federal exemptions allowed
	New York code
	NY Civil Practice Law
Homestead	5206(A)
	NY Debtor and Creditor Law
Car	282(1)
	NY Civil Practice Law
Personal property	5205(A)(1)-(9)
	NY Ins Law
Life insurance	3212(B)
	NY Debtor and Creditor Law
Tools of trade	282(2)(E)
	NY Civil Practice Law
Wild card	5205(A)(1)-(9)
	NY Civil Practice Law
	5205(A)(9)

North Carolina	No federal exemptions allowed
	North Carolina code
Homestead	1C-1601 (A)(1)
Car	1C-1601 (A)(3)
Personal property	1C-1601 (A)(4)
Life insurance	1C-1601 (A)(6)
Tools of trade	1C-1601 (A)(5)
Wild card	1C-1601 (A)(2)

North Dakota	No federal exemptions allowed
	North Dakota code
Homestead	28-22-02(10); 47-18-01
	$100,000
Car	28-22-03.1(1)
Personal property	28-22-02(1)-(8); 28-22-03.1(2); (4)
	(A); (B); 28-22-03; 28-22-04(1)(4);
	28-22-05
Life insurance	33-40:26.1-33-40
Tools of trade	28-22-03.1(4)(A)
Wild card	See personal property
Ohio	No federal exemptions allowed
	Ohio code
	2329.66(A)(1)(B)
Homestead	2329.66(A)(2)(B)
Car	2329.66(A)(3)-(12)
Personal property	2329.66(A)(6)(A);(B);3911.12;14
Life insurance	2329.66(A)(4)(B);(C);(D)
Tools of trade	2329.66(A)(4)(B);(C);(D)
Wild card	
Oklahoma	No federal exemptions allowed
	Oklahoma code
Homestead	31-1 (A)(1); 31-1 (A)(2); 31-2
Car	31-1 (A)(13)
Personal property	31-1 (A)(3)-(21)
Tools of trade	31-1(A)(5);(6); 31-1(C)
Wild card	None
Oregon	No federal exemptions allowed
	Oregon code
Homestead	23.164; 23.240; 23.250
Car	23.160(1)(K)
Personal property	23.160(1)(A)-(N)
Life insurance	743.046
Tools of trade	23.160(1)(C)
Wild card	$400 of any personal property

Pennsylvania

Federal exemptions allowed
Pennsylvania code

Homestead	None
Car	None
Personal property	42-8124(A)-(4)
Life insurance	42-8124(C)(3);(4);(6)
Tools of trade	None
Wild card	42-8123

Rhode Island

Federal exemptions allowed
Rhode Island code

Homestead	9-26-4.1
Car	None
Personal property	9-26-4(1)-(7)
Life insurance	27-4-12
Tools of trade	9-26-4(2)
Wild card	None

South Carolina

No federal exemptions allowed
South Carolina code

Homestead	15-41-30(1)
Car	15-41-30(2)
Personal property	15-41-30(1)-(9)
Life insurance	38-38-330; 15-41-30(8); (11)(c)
Tools of trade	15-41-30(6)
Wild card	None

South Dakota

No federal exemptions
South Dakota code

Homestead	43-31-1(1);(2);(3);(4); 43-45-3
Car	None
Personal property	43-45-2;4;5; 43-45-5(1)-(5)
Life insurance	58-15-70; 43-45-6
Tools of trade	See personal property
Wild card	See personal property

Tennessee	No federal exemptions allowed
	Tennessee code
Homestead	26-2-301; 26-2-302; 26-2-303
	$5,000; $7,500
Car	None
Personal property	26-2-111(2)(B);(C);(3);(5)
Life insurance	56-7-03
Tools of trade	26-2-111(4)
Wild card	26-2-102
Texas	Federal exemptions allowed
	Texas code
Homestead	Tex. Property 41.001; 41.002
	Unlimited
Car	42.001:42.002
Personal property	42.001:42.002
Life insurance	42.002(A)(12)
Tools of trade	42.002(A)(3);(4)
Wild card	None
Utah	No federal exemptions allowed
	Utah code
Homestead	78-23-3:78-23-4
Car	78-23-8(2)
Personal property	78-23-8(1)(A);(B);(C);(2)
Life insurance	31A-9-603; 78-23-7
Tools of trade	39-1-47; 78-23-8(3)
Wild card	None
Vermont	Federal exemptions allowed
	Vermont code
Homestead	27-101:27-105:12-2740(19)(D)
Car	12-2740(3)
Personal property	12-2740(3)-(19)
Life insurance	8-3706:8-3705:12-2740(18):(19)(H)
Tools of trade	12-2740(2)
Wild card	12-2740(7)

Virginia	No federal exemptions allowed
	Virginia code
Homestead	34-4; 34-18; 34-20
	$5,000
Car	34-26(8)
Personal property	34-26(1)-(8)
Life insurance	38.2-3339
Tools of trade	34-26; 44-96
Wild card	34-4.1

Washington	Federal exemptions allowed
	Washington code
Homestead	6.13.010; 6.13.030; 6.15.040
Car	6.15.010(3)(F)
Personal property	6.15.010(1)-(3)
Life insurance	48.18.410
Tools of trade	6.15.010(4)(A);(B);(C)
Wild card	6.15.010(3)(B)

West Virginia	No federal exemptions allowed
	West Virginia code
	38-10-4(A)
Homestead	$25,000
	38-10-4(B)
Car	$2,400
	38-10-4(A)-(K)
Personal property	33-6-28;38-10-4(G);(H);(K)(3)
Life insurance	38-10-4(F)
Tools of trade	38-10-4(E)
Wild card	

Wisconsin	Federal exemptions allowed Wisconsin code
Homestead	815.20 $75,000
Car	815.18(3)(G) $4,000
Personal property	815.18(3)(D) $12,000
Life insurance	815.18(3)(i)(1)(a)
Tools of trade	815.18(3)(B) $15,000
Wild card	815.18(3)(G) 73

Wyoming	No federal exemptions allowed Wyoming code
Homestead	1-20-101; 1-20-102; 1-20-103; 1-20-104
Car	$20,000
Personal property	1-20-106(A)(iv) 1-20-106(A)(i)-(iv); 1-20-105;
Life insurance	26-32-102;
Tools of trade	35-8-104
Wild card	26-15-133 1-20-106(6) None

Means Test Information

Census Bureau's Median Family Income by Family Size

The following table provides median family income data reproduced in a format designed for ease of use in completing Bankruptcy Form 122A-1.

| State | 1 Earner | Family size | | |
		2 People	3 People	4 People*
Alabama	$48,544	$56,918	$68,554	$82,991
Alaska	$63,997	$77,589	$102,315	$103,055
Arizona	$52,319	$65,713	$71,704	$86,950
Arkansas	$4,323c	$53,946	$58,258	$74,086
California	$6,036c	$79,271	$88,235	$101,315
Colorado	$6,192*	$81,155	$94,193	$107,867
Connecticut	$66,685	$88,594	$101,666	$125,714
Delaware	$55,578	$72,644	$84,584	$102,625
District of Columbia	$63,414	$115,082	$129,777	$140,615
Florida	$51,559	$62,736	$68,944	$82,560
Georgia	$50,128	$65,007	$73,738	$87,317
Hawaii	$65,977	$77,621	$100,620	$114,381
Idaho	$52,117	$61,916	$67,422	$77,923
Illinois	$54,877	$72,593	$83,759	$103,074
Indiana	$48,834	$62,931	$73,537	$87,636

Iowa	$51,579	$69,127	$78,930	$95,581
Kansas	$51,867	$67,221	$76,999	$88,698
Kentucky	$44,594	$56,257	$66,732	$80,115
Louisiana	$45,634	$55,410	$63,039	$82,282
Maine	$51,453	$64,889	$78,379	$95,614
Maryland	$70,789	$90,424	$106,282	$128,272
Massachusetts	$67,119	$84,125	$108,130	$134,418
Michigan	$53,113	$64 428	$78,217	$93,653
Minnesota	$58,050	$77,702	$97,657	$114,326
Mississippi	$42,414	$51 904	$58,472	$69,732
Missouri	$49,086	$61,519	$73,857	$92,129
Montana	$51,074	$64,425	$74,919	$87,293
Nebraska	$49,680	$69,294	$78,674	$95,445
Nevada	$52,449	$65,756	$74,856	$81,528
New Hampshire	$66,585	$80,429	$102,095	$122,523
New Jersey	$69,705	$83,739	$106,650	$131,331
New Mexico	$45,645	$56,327	$60,617	$67,560
New York	$57,137	$72,642	$88,240	$107,550
North Carolina	$48,772	$62,050	$69,162	$87,505
North Dakota	$53,306	$80,899	$87,824	$99,327
Ohio	$51,297	$64,669	$77,642	$93,239
Oklahoma	$49,198	$59,495	$66,585	$76,691
Oregon	$56,957	$71,838	$80,698	$99,074
Pennsylvania	$54,605	$67,540	$83,868	$103,316
Rhode Island	$61,706	$75,858	$85,100	$104,833
South Carolina	$47,487	$61,529	$66,595	$81,226
South Dakota	$47,906	$69,046	$70,326	$83,823
Tennessee	$48,219	$60,913	$69,734	$79,701
Texas	$50,902	$66,899	$73,948	$86,259
Utah	$64,806	$69,006	$82,638	$93,474
Vermont	$57,859	$75,602	$81,686	$103,627

Virginia	$62,029	$79,412	$91,995	$111,993
Washington	$67,511	$80,251	$92,568	$107,481
West Virginia	$49,056	$52,028	$64,281	$76,273
Wisconsin	$52,730	$68,363	$83,607	$100,098
Wyoming	$62,090	$74,286	$78,310	$97,862

Add $9,000 for each individual in excess of four.

Commonwealth or US territory	1 Earner	Family size		
		2 People	3 People	4 People*
Guam	$42,770	$51,139	$58,275	$70,520
Northern Mariana Islands	$28,722	$28,722	$33,416	$49,148
Puerto Rico	$24,701	$24,701	$26,023	$34,108
Virgin Islands	$33,935	$40,785	$43,486	$47,642

Add $9,000 for each individual in excess of four.

Approved Credit-Counseling Agencies

Approved Credit-Counseling Agencies

Main address:
2711 E. Melrose Street
Gilbert, AZ 85297
877-376-7122

Delivery method:

Internet:

www.
myonlinebankruptcyclass.
com

www.
myonlinebankruptcyclass.
com

English and Spanish

Main address:
304 S Jones Boulevard
Suite 1027
Las Vegas, NV 89107
856-742-6259

Delivery method:

Internet:

www.simpleclass.net

www.simpleclass.net

Main address:
378 Summit Avenue
Jersey City, NJ 07305
1-800-610-3920

Delivery method:

Internet:

www.debtorcc.org

www.debtorcc.org

English and Spanish

Main address:
1400 Preston
Road Suite 499
Plano, TX 75093
800-496-2440

Delivery method:

Internet:	www.1dollarwiser.come	
Telephone:	800-496-2440	www.1dollarwiser.come

Main address:
1000 NW 57th Court
Suite 860
Miami, FL 33126
305-269-9201

www.a123cc.org

Delivery method:

Internet:	www.a123cc.org	*English and Spanish*
Telephone:	1-888-412-2123	*English and Spanish*

1stopbk.com Inc.
Main address:
362 Sweetbriar Lane
Lakeland, FL 33813
888-988-3410

Delivery method:

Internet:	www.1stopbk.com	www.1stopbk.com

Abacus Credit
Counseling
Main address:
17337 Ventura
Boulevard
Suite 205
Encino, CA 91316
800-516-3834

www.abacuscc.org

Delivery method:
Internet: www.abacuscc.org *English and Spanish*
Telephone: 800-516-3834 *English and Spanish*

Access Counseling Inc.
Main address:
633 W. 5th Street
Suite 26001
Los Angeles, CA 90071
800-205-9297

www.accesscounselinginc.
org

Delivery method:
Internet: www.accesscounseling.com *English and Spanish*
Telephone: 800-205-9297 *English and Spanish*

Advantage Credit
Counseling Service Inc.
Main address:
River Park Commons
2403 Sidney Street,
Suite 400
Pittsburgh, PA 15203
888-511-2227

Delivery method:
   Internet: www.advantageccs.org
   Telephone: 866-409-2227   www.advantageccs.org

Alien Credit and Debt
Counseling Agency
Main address:
20003 387th Avenue
Wolsey, SD 57384
888-415-8173

                                      www.acdcas.com

Delivery method:
   Internet: www.acdcas.com   *English and Spanish*
   Telephone: 888-415-8173   *English and Spanish*

Alliance Credit
Counseling Inc.
Main address:
10720 Sikes Place
Suite 100
Charlotte, NC 28277
888-594-9594

                                        www.knowdebt.org

Delivery method:
   Internet: www.knowdebt.org   *English and Spanish*
   Telephone: 888-594-9596   *English and Spanish*

American Consumer
Credit Counseling Inc.
Main address:
130 Rumford Avenue
Suite 202
Newton, MA 02466
866-826-6924

www.ConsumerCredit.org

Delivery method:

Internet:	www.consumercredit.org	*English and Spanish*
Telephone:	1-866-826-6924	*English and Spanish*

American Debt
Resources Inc.
Main address:
384 Larkfield Road
East Northport,
NY 11731
800-498-0766

www.
americandebtresources.com

Delivery method:

Telephone:	800-498-0766	*English and Spanish*

American Financial
Solutions of North
Seattle Community
College Foundation
Main address:
600 University Street
Suite 2409
Seattle, WA 98121
800-894-7240

Delivery method:
Internet:
Telephone:

www.myfinacialgoals.org

1-800-894-7240

www.myfinacialgoals.org

English and Spanish

Aurora Family
Service Inc.
Main address:
3200 W Highland
Blvd.
Milwaukee, WI 53208
414-482-8801

Delivery method:
In person:

Consumer Credit
Counseling Service of
Greater Milwaukee
3200 W Highland Blvd
Milwaukee, WI 53208
414-482-8801
Consumer Credit
Counseling Service of
Greater Milwaukee
101 W Broadway
Waukesha, WI 53186
414-482-8801
Consumer Credit
Counseling Service of
Greater Milwaukee
4025 N 92nd
Avenue Suite #25
Wauwatosa, WI 53226
414-482-8801

www.creditcounselingwi.org

Black Hills Children's
Ranch Inc.
Main address:
1644 Concourse Drive
Rapid City, SD 57703
605-348-1608

www.pioneercredit.com

Delivery method:
Internet: www.pioneercredit.com   *English and Spanish*
Telephone: 800-888-1596   *English and Spanish*

Cambridge Credit
Counseling Corp.
Main address:
67 Hunt Street
Agawam, MA 01001
800-403-3433

Delivery method:
Internet: www.cambridgecredit.org
Telephone: 8004033433   www.cambridge-credit.org

Catholic Charities
Budget Counseling
1825 Riverside Drive
Green Bay, WI 54301
920-437-7531
English and Spanish
(interpreter only)

Catholic Charities
Budget Counseling
206 N. 8th Street
Manitowoc, WI 54220
920-684-6651
English and Spanish
(interpreter only)

Catholic Charities of the
Diocese of Green Bay Inc.
d/b/a Catholic Charities
Budget Counseling
1712 Dunlap Ave Ste 5
Marinette, WI 54143
715-735-7802
English and Spanish

Catholic Charities of the
Diocese of Green Bay Inc.
1475 Opportunity Way
Menasha, WI 54952
920-738-9635
English and Spanish

Catholic Charities
of the Diocese of
Green Bay Inc.
Main address:
1825 Riverside Drive
Green Bay, WI 54301
920-272-8234

Delivery method:
In person:

www.newcatholiccharities.
org

CC Advising Inc.
Main address:
703 Washington Ave.
Suite 200
Bay City, MI
48708-5732
1-855-980-6690

www.ccadvising.com

Delivery method:
Internet: www.ccadvising.com *English and Spanish*

Consumer Credit
Counseling Service
of Buffalo Inc.
Main address:
40 Gardenville Parkway
Suite 300
West Seneca, NY 14224
716-712-2060

www.
consumercreditbuffalo.org

Delivery method:
Telephone: 800-926-9685 *English and Spanish*

Consumer Credit
Counseling Service of
Northeastern Iowa Inc.
Main address:
1003 West 4th Street
Waterloo, IA 50702
319-234-0661

Delivery method:
Telephone: 800-714-4388 www.cccsia.org

Consumer Credit
Counseling Service
of the Midwest Inc.
Main address:
690 Taylor Road
Suite 150
Gahanna, OH 43230
800-355-2227

Delivery method: www.apprisen.com
    Telephone: 800-355-2227   *English and Spanish*

Consumer Credit
Counseling Services
of Maryland and
Delaware Inc.
Main address:
6315 Hillside Court
Suite B
Columbia, MD 21046
410-747-2050

Delivery method:
    Internet: www.cccsmd.org
    Telephone: 800-642-2227   www.cccsmd.org

Consumer Education
Services Inc. d/b/a
Start Fresh Today
Main address:
3700 Barrett Drive
Raleigh, NC 27609
919-785-0725

www.startfreshtoday.com

Delivery method:

Internet:	www.startfreshtoday.com	*English and Spanish*
Telephone:	800-435-9138	*English and Spanish*

Credit Advisors
Foundation
Main address:
1818 South 72nd Street
Omaha, NE 68124
402-393-3100

www.creditadvisors.org;

Delivery method: Internet:	www. yourbankruptcypartner. com	www. yourbankruptcypartner.com
Telephone:	800-625-775	*English and Spanish*

Credit Card
Management
Services Inc. d/b/a
Debthelper.com
Main address:
1325 N. Congress Ave.
Suite 201
West Palm Beach,
FL 33401
800-920-2262

www.debthelper.com

Delivery method:
    Internet: www.debthelper.com   *English and Spanish*
    Telephone: 800-920-2262   *English and Spanish*

Credit Counseling
Center
Main address:
832 Second Street Pike
Richboro, PA 18954
215-348-8003

Delivery method:
    Internet: www.ccc-credit.com
    Telephone: 877-900-4222   www.ccc-credit.com

Cricket Debt
Counseling
Main address:
219 SW Stark Street
Suite 200
Portland, OR 97204
503-353-0400

www.cricketdebt.com

Delivery method:		
Internet:	www.cricketdebt.com	*English and Spanish*
Telephone:	866-719-0400	*English and Spanish*

Debt Counseling Corp.
Main address:
3033 Express
Drive North
Suite 103
Hauppauge, NY 11749
888-354-6332

www.debtcounselingcorp.
org

Delivery method:	www.debtcounselingcorp.	
Internet:	org	*English and Spanish*

Debt Education
and Certification
Foundation
Main address:
112 Goliad Street
Benbrook, TX 76126
866-859-7323

www.bkcert.com

Delivery method:		
Internet:	www.bkcert.com	*English and Spanish*
Telephone:	866-859-7323	*English and Spanish*

Debt Management
Credit Counseling
Corp.
Main address:
3310 N. Federal
Highway
Lighthouse Point,
FL 33064
954-418-1466

Delivery method:		www.dmcccorp.org
Internet:	www.dmcccorp.org	
Telephone:	888-777-0981	*English and Spanish*

Debt Reduction
Services Inc.
Main address:
6213 N. Cloverdale
Road
Suite 100
Boise, ID 83713
208-378-0200

www.debtreductionservices.
org

Delivery method:	www.	
Internet:	debtreductionservices.org	*English and Spanish*

Dollar Learning
Foundation Inc.
Main address:
21550 Oxnard Street
3rd Floor PMB #001
Woodland Hills,
CA 91367
877-366-6070

www.dollarbk.org

Delivery method:
   Internet: www.dollarbk.org   *English and Spanish*
   Telephone: 877-366-6070   *English and Spanish*

Evergreen Financial
Counseling
Main address:
2156 Church St. SE
Salem, OR 97302
800-581-3513

Delivery method:
   Internet: www.evergreenclass.com
   Telephone: 800-581-3513   www.evergreenclass.com

Family Financial
Education Foundation
Main address:
724 Front Street
Suite 340
Evanston, WY 82930
307-789-2010

www.ffef.org

Delivery method:
   Internet: www.ffef.org
   Telephone: 307-789-2010   *English and Spanish*

800-350-2227

Family Service
Association of
Sheboygan Inc.
Main address:
1930 N. 8th Street
Sheboygan, WI 53081
920-458-3784

Delivery method:
Telephone:
In person:

CCCS of Fond du Lac
17 Forest Avenue Suite 016
Fond Du Lac, WI 54935
800-350-2227
CCCS of Sheboygan
1930 N. 8th Street
Sheboygan, WI 53081
920-458-3784
CCCS of West Bend
139 N. Main Street
Suite 101
West Bend, WI 53095
262-306-9241

www.cccsonline.org

www.fisc-cccs.org
1-800-366-8161
Consumer Credit
Counseling Service
of NE Wisconsin
1600 W. Mason Street
Green Bay, WI 54303

Financial Information
& Service Center Inc.
Main address:
1800 Appleton Road
Menasha, WI 54952
920-886-1000

920-569-8596
Consumer Credit
Counseling Service
of NE Wisconsin
1800 Appleton Road
Menasha, WI 54952
920-886-1000

Delivery method:
Internet:
Telephone:
In person:

Consumer Credit
Counseling Service
of NE Wisconsin
1600 W. 20th Street
Oshkosh, WI 54902
920-966-1200
Consumer Credit
Counseling Service
of NE Wisconsin
57 N. 12th Avenue
Sturgeon Bay, WI 54235
920-743-1862

www.fisc-cccs.org

Garden State
Consumer Credit
Counseling Inc. d/b/a
Navicore Solutions
Main address:
200 US, Highway 9
Manalapan, NJ 07726
732-409-6281

www.navicoresolutions.org

Delivery method:
Internet: www.navicoresolutions.org   *English and Spanish*

GreenPath Inc.
d/b/a GreenPath
Financial Wellness
Main address:
36500 Corporate Drive
Farmington Hills,
MI 48331
800-630-6718

www.greenpath.org

Delivery method:
Internet: www.greenpath.org   *English and Spanish*
Telephone: 800-630-6718   *English and Spanish*

Hananwill Credit
Counseling
Main address:
115 North Cross Street
Robinson, IL 62454
877-544-5560

Delivery method:
Internet: www.hananwill.com
Telephone: 877-544-5560   www.hananwill.com

InCharge Debt
Solutions
Main address:
5750 Major Blvd
Suite 300
Orlando, FL 32819
407-532-5716

Delivery method:
Internet:
Telephone:

www.
personalfinanceeducation.
com
1-407-532-5716

www.
personalfinanceeducation.
com

English and Spanish
English and Spanish

Money Management
International Inc.
Main address:
14141 Southwest
Freeway
Suite 1000
Sugar Land, TX
77478-3494
(877) 964-2227

Delivery method:
Internet:
Telephone:

www.moneymanagement.
org
(877) 964-2227

www.moneymanagement.
org

English and Spanish
English and Spanish

MoneySharp Credit
Counseling Inc.
Main address:
1916 N. Fairfield
Avenue
Suite 2
Chicago, IL 60647
866-200-6825

www.moneysharp.org

Delivery method:
Internet: www.moneysharp.org   *English and Spanish*

National Debt
Management Inc.
Main address:
17520 West 12
Mile Road
Suite 105
Southfield, MI 48076
248-200-2106

Delivery method:
Internet: www.nationaldebtmgt.com
Telephone: 1-855-378-8989   www.nationaldebtmgt.com

SafeGuard Credit
Counseling
Services Inc.
Main address:
67 Fort Salonga Road
Northport, NY 11768
800-673-6993

Delivery method:		www.safeguardcredit.org
Internet:	www.safeguardcredit.org	
Telephone:	800-673-6993	*English and Spanish*

Springboard Nonprofit
Consumer Credit
Management Inc.,
d/b/a credit.org
Main address:
4351 Latham Street
Riverside, CA 92501
951-781-0114

		www.bkhelp.org
Delivery method:	www.bkhelp.org or	
Internet:	www.bancarrota.org	*English and Spanish*
Telephone:	888-425-3452	*English and Spanish*

Stand Sure Credit
Counseling, aka Biblical
Financial Concepts Inc.
Main address:
406 5th Street North
Suite 1
Oneonta, AL 35121
877-240-1398

Delivery method:
    Internet: www.standsurecc.org
    Telephone: 877-240-1398   www.standsurecc.org

Summit Financial
Education Inc.
Main address:
4800 E. Flower Street
Tucson, AZ 85712
1-800-780-5965

                                    www.summitfe.org

Delivery method:
    Internet: www.SummitFE.org   *English and Spanish*
    Telephone: 1-800-780-5965   *English and Spanish*

Take Charge
America Inc.
Main address:
20620 North
19th Avenue
Phoenix, AZ
85027-3585
623-266-6100

                              www.takechargeamerica.org

Delivery method:
    Internet: bankruptcycounseling.org/   *English and Spanish*

The Kingdom
Ministries Inc.
Main address:
6094 Apple Tree Drive
Suite 1
Memphis, TN 38115
901-552-5131

Delivery method: www.thekingdomminitries.
  Telephone: 901-552-5131   com

Urgent Credit
Counseling Inc.
Main address:
219 SW Stark Street
Suite 200
Portland, OR 97204
866-233-1940

                                                                         www.urgentco.com
Delivery method:
  Internet: www.urgentco.com   *English and Spanish*
  Telephone: 866-233-1940   *English and Spanish*

WIW
Western District
of Wisconsin
$$$$$$0$ BK
Class Inc.
Main address:
2711 E. Melrose Street
Gilbert, AZ 85297   www.
877-376-7122   myonlinebankruptcyclass.
                                          www.   com
Delivery method: myonlinebankruptcyclass.
  Internet: com   *English and Spanish*

$$$$$Simple Class Inc.
Main address:
304 S Jones Boulevard
Suite 1027
Las Vegas, NV 89107
866-742-6259

Delivery method:
Internet: www.simpleclass.net   www.simpleclass.net

001 Debtorcc Inc.
Main address:
378 Summit Avenue
Jersey City, NJ 07306
1-800-610-3920

                                                      www.debtorcc.org

Delivery method:
Internet: www.debtorcc.org   *English and Spanish*

1$ Wiser Consumer
Education Inc.
Main address:
1400 Preston
Road Suite 499
Plano, TX 75093
800-496-2440

Delivery method:
Internet: www.1dollarwiser.com
Telephone: 800-496-2440   www.1dollarwiser.com

123 Credit
Counselors Inc
Main address:
1000 NW 57th Court
Suite 860
Miami, FL 33126
305-269-9201

www.a123cc.org

Delivery method:
    Internet: www.a123cc.org   *English and Spanish*
    Telephone: 1-888-412-2123   *English and Spanish*

1stopbk.com Inc.
Main address:
362 Sweetbriar Lane
Lakeland, FL 33813
888-988-3410

Delivery method:
    Internet: www.1stopbk.com   www.1stopbk.com

Abacus Credit
Counseling
Main address:
17337 Ventura
Boulevard
Suite 205
Encino, CA 91316
800-516-3834

www.abacuscc.org

Delivery method:
    Internet: www.abacuscc.org   *English and Spanish*
    Telephone: 800-516-3834   *English and Spanish*

Access Counseling Inc.
Main address:
633 W. 5th Street
Suite 26001
Los Angeles, CA 90071
800-205-9297

www.accesscounselinginc.
org

Delivery method:	www.accesscounselinginc.	
Internet:	org	*English and Spanish*
Telephone:	800-205-9297	*English and Spanish*

Advantage Credit
Counseling Service Inc.
Main address:
River Park Commons
2403 Sidney Street,
Suite 400
Pittsburgh, PA 15203
888-511-2227

Delivery method:		
Internet:	www.advantageccs.org	
Telephone:	866-409-2227	www.advantageccs.org

Allen Credit and Debt
Counseling Agency
Main address:
20003 387th Avenue
Wolsey, SD 57384
888-415-8173

www.acdcas.com

Delivery method:		
Internet:	www.acdcas.com	*English and Spanish*
Telephone:	888-415-8173	*English and Spanish*

Alliance Credit
Counseling Inc.
Main address:
10720 Sikes Place
Suite 100
Charlotte, NC 28277
888-594-9594

www.knowdebt.org

Delivery method:

Internet:	www.knowdebt.org	*English and Spanish*
Telephone:	888-594-9596	*English and Spanish*

American Consumer
Credit Counseling Inc.
Main address:
130 Rumford Avenue
Suite 202
Newton, MA 02466
866-826-6924

www.ConsumerCredit.org

Delivery method:

Internet:	www.consumercredit.org	*English and Spanish*
Telephone:	1-866-826-6924	*English and Spanish*

American Debt
Resources Inc.
Main address:
384 Larkfield Road
East Northport,
NY 11731
800-498-0766

www.
americandebtresources.com

Delivery method:

Telephone:	800-498-0766	*English and Spanish*

American Financial
Solutions of North
Seattle Community
College Foundation
Main address:
600 University Street
Suite 2409
Seattle, WA 98121
800-894-7240

Delivery method:		www.myfinancialgoals.org
Internet:	www.myfinancialgoals.org	
Telephone:	1-800-894-7240	*English and Spanish*

Aurora Family
Services Inc.
Main address:
3200 W Highland
Blvd.
Milwaukee, WI 53208
414-482-8801

| Delivery method: | | www.creditcounselingwi.org |

Black Hills Children's
Ranch Inc.
Main address:
1644 Concourse Drive
Rapid City, SD 57703
605-348-1608

		www.pioneercredit.com
Delivery method:		
Internet:	www.pioneercredit.com	*English and Spanish*
Telephone:	800-888-1596	*English and Spanish*

Cambridge Credit
Counseling Corp.
Main address:
67 Hunt Street
Agawam, MA 01001
800-403-3433

Delivery method:
    Internet: www.cambridgecredit.org
    Telephone: 8004033433 www.cambridge-credit.org

CC Advising Inc.
Main address:
703 Washington Ave.
Suite 200
Bay City, MI
48708-5732
1-855-980-6690

www.ccadvising.com

Delivery method:
    Internet: www.ccadvising.com *English and Spanish*

Consumer Credit
Counseling Service
of Buffalo Inc.
Main address:
40 Gardenville Parkway
Suite 300
West Seneca, NY 14224
716-712-2060

www.
consumercreditbuffalo.org

Delivery method:
    Telephone: 800-926-9685 *English and Spanish*

Consumer Credit
Counseling Service
of the Midwest Inc.
Main address:
690 Taylor Road
Suite 150
Gahanna, OH 43230
800-355-2227

www.apprisen.com

Delivery method:
Telephone: 800-355-2227 *English and Spanish*

Consumer Credit
Counseling Service
of Maryland and
Delaware Inc.
Main address:
6315 Hillside Court
Suite B
Columbia, MD 21046
410-747-2050

Delivery method:
Internet: www.cccsmd.org
Telephone: 800-642-2227 www.cccsmd.org

Consumer Education Services Inc., d/b/a Start Fresh Today
Main address:
3700 Barrett Drive
Raleigh, NC 27609
919-785-0725

www.startfreshtoday.com

Delivery method:		
Internet:	www.startfreshtoday.com	*English and Spanish*
Telephone:	800-435-9138	*English and Spanish*

Credit Advisors Foundation
Main address:
1818 South 72nd Street
Omaha, NE 68124
402-393-3100

www.creditadvisors.org;

Delivery method:	www.yourbankruptcypartner.com	www.yourbankruptcypartner.com
Internet:		
Telephone:	800-625-7725	*English and Spanish*

Credit Card
Management
Services Inc. d/b/a
Debthelper.com
Main address:
1325 N. Congress Ave.
Suite 201
West Palm Beach,
FL 33401
800-920-2262

www.debthelper.com

Delivery method:
Internet: www.debthelper.com   *English and Spanish*
Telephone: 800-920-2262   *English and Spanish*

Credit Counseling
Center
Main address:
8332 Second
Street Pike
Richboro, PA 18954
215-348-8003

Delivery method:
Internet: www.ccc-credit.com
Telephone: 877-900-4222   www.ccc-credit.com

Cricket Debt
Counseling
Main address:
219 SW Stark Street
Suite 200
Portland, OR 97204
503-353-0400

www.cricketdebt.com

Delivery method:		
Internet:	www.cricketdebt.com	*English and Spanish*
Telephone:	866-719-0400	*English and Spanish*

Debt Counseling Corp.
Main address:
3033 Express
Drive North
Suite 103
Hauppauge, NY 11749
888-354-6332

www.debtcounselingcorp.
org

Delivery method:	www.debtcounselingcorp.	
Internet:	org	*English and Spanish*

Debt Education
and Certification
Foundation
Main address:
112 Goliad Street
Benbrook, TX 76126
866-859-7323

www.bkcert.com

Delivery method:		
Internet:	www.bkcert.com	*English and Spanish*
Telephone:	866-859-7323	*English and Spanish*

Debt Management
Credit Counseling
Corp.
Main address:
3310 N. Federal
Highway
Lighthouse Point,
FL 33064
954-418-1466

Delivery method:		www.dmcccorp.org
Internet:	www.dmcccorp.org	
Telephone:	888-777-0981	*English and Spanish*

Debt Reduction
Services Inc.
Main address:
6213 N. Cloverdale
Road
Suite 100
Boise, ID 83713
208-378-0200

		www.debtreductionservices.org
Delivery method:	www.	
Internet:	debtreductionservices.org	*English and Spanish*

Dollar Learning
Foundation Inc.
Main address:
21550 Oxnard Street
3rd Floor PMB #001
Woodland Hills,
CA 91387
877-366-6070

Delivery method:

www.dollarbk.org

Internet:	www.dollarbk.org	*English and Spanish*
Telephone:	877-366-6070	*English and Spanish*

Evergreen Financial
Counseling
Main address:
2156 Church St. SE
Salem, OR 97302
800-581-3513

Delivery method:

Internet:	www.evergreenclass.com	
Telephone:	800-581-3513	www.evergreenclass.com

Family Financial
Education Foundation
Main address:
724 Front Street
Suite 340
Evanston, WY 82930
307-789-2010

Delivery method:

www.ffef.org

Internet:	www.ffef.org	
Telephone:	307-789-2010	*English and Spanish*

Family Service
Association of
Sheboygan Inc.
Main address:
1930 N. 8th Street
Sheboygan, WI 53081
920-458-3784

800-350-2227
CCCS of LaCrosse
Delivery method: 505 King Street Suite 212
Telephone: LaCrosse, WI 54601
In person: 608-784-8380 www.cccsonline.org

Financial Information
& Service Center Inc.
Main address:
1800 Appleton Road
Menasha, WI 54952
920-886-1000

Delivery method:
Internet: www.fisc-cccs.org
Telephone: 1-800-366-8161 www.fisc-cccs.org

Garden State
Consumer Credit
Counseling Inc., d/b/a
Navicore Solutions
Main address:
200 US, Highway 9
Manalapan, NJ 07726
732-409-6281

www.navicoresolutions.org
Delivery method:
Internet: www.navicoresolutions.org *English and Spanish*

GreenPath Inc.
d/b/a GreenPath
Financial Wellness
Main address:

Delivery method:
   Internet: www.nationaldebtmgt.com
   Telephone: 1-855-378-8989   www.greenpath.org

SafeGuard Credit
Counseling Services Inc
Main address:
67 Fort Salonga Road
Northport, NY 11768
800-673-6993

Delivery method: www.safeguardcredit.org
   Internet: www.safeguardcredit.org
   Telephone: 800-673-6993   *English and Spanish*

Springboard Nonprofit
Consumer Credit
Management Inc.,
d/b/a credit.org
Main address:
4351 Latham Street
Riverside, CA 92501
951-781-0114

Delivery method: www.bkhelp.org
   Internet: www.bkhelp.org or www.bancarrota.org   *English and Spanish*
   Telephone: 888-425-3452   *English and Spanish*

Stand Sure Credit
Counseling, aka Biblical
Financial Concepts Inc.
Main address:
406 5th Street North
Suite 1
Oneonta, AL 35121
877-240-1398

Delivery method:
   Internet: www.standsurecc.org
   Telephone: 877-240-1398   www.standsurecc.org

Summit Financial
Education Inc.
Main address:
4800 E. Power Street
Tucson, AZ 85712
1-800-780-5965

                                 www.summitfe.org

Delivery method:
   Internet: www.summitFE.org   *English and Spanish*
   Telephone: 1-800-780-5965   *English and Spanish*

Take Charge
America Inc.
Main address:
20620 North
19th Avenue
Phoenix, AZ
65027-3585
623-266-6100

                          www.takechargeamerica.org

Delivery method: bankcruptcycounseling.
   Internet: org/   English and Spanish

The Kingdom
Ministries Inc.
Main address:
6094 Apple Tree Drive
Suite 1
Memphis, TN 38115
901-552-5131

Delivery method:		www.
Telephone:	901-552-5131	thekingdomministries.com

Urgent Credit
Counseling Inc.
Main address:
219 SW Stark Street
Suite 200
Portland, OR 97204
866-233-1940

		www.urgentco.com
Delivery method:		
Internet:	www.urgentco.com	English and Spanish
Telephone:	866-233-1940	English and Spanish

USTP Home | Approved Credit-Counseling Agencies | Notice
and Disclaimers | FOIA | Privacy Policy | DOJ Home

Stephen Lee has been assisting anyone who chooses self-representation and wants to file their own bankruptcy for over twenty years. He has also assisted persons in administrative advocacy, preparing for administrative hearings, employment relations, wage payments, personnel records, wrongful discharge, and uncontested divorce without minor children.

CPSIA information can be obtained
at www.ICGtesting.com
Printed in the USA
LVHW101227090223
738979LV00019B/475

9 781685 706142